A Love Letter To Ukraine

Margie Ann Wright

BookLeaf Publishing

India | USA | UK

Presentation by *BookLeaf Publishing*

Web: www.bookleafpub.com

E-mail: info@bookleafpub.com

ISBN: 9789358316469

First edition 2023

DEDICATION

For Jeff Abrams, who has given his life, his fortune, and his sacred honor to keep the whole of Ukraine alive and well and thriving in the face of evil. His unfailing commitment to the church in Ukraine has kept it safe, healthy, and growing. I suppose if it were possible, he would open his veins to put an end to the heartbreaks and terrors of this war. May God bless him with a special measure of strength and tenacity for the days ahead.

ACKNOWLEDGEMENT

I'd like to thank Oleksandr Rodichev (Sasha) for befriending me in the earliest days of the struggle and keeping me up to date on all things Ukraine. He shared his friends, his family, his church and his homeland with me. He, Dmytro, Stas, Bohdan Yasinskyi, along with Dennis, Konstantin, and the Bila Tserkva team have kept company with me in days when their time and energy were precious commodities not lightly spent. Their ability to befriend, love, and encourage a complete stranger while facing the most trying times of their lives is remarkable and will never be forgotten. The Volunteer Brothers, as well as Ann Nazarenko, never fail to lift my spirits and serve as purveyors of hope to all those they encounter.

All these valiant warriors of peace have served as a rescue squad arriving in my life, a million miles away in a little town in East Texas, at a time when I really needed an infusion of hope. They share with me their faith in a world worth saving, and in turn, renew my weary heart on a daily basis. May the Lord our God guide, guard, and protect each and every one of them as they navigate a world gone mad.

PREFACE

When war broke out in Ukraine, I was a student of creative writing at Oxford. I found it almost impossible to write about anything except the struggles in Ukraine. I wound up writing poems, plays, prose, and movie scripts that bore witness to the heartbreaking events as they unfolded. Most of it now lives in the Oxford archives along with other work from my two years at the university. Though I have tried to move on to other people, places, and events with my writing, my heart has made it evident that until I pay homage to the love I feel for Ukraine, I will be haunted by the names and faces of her people. And so I have picked up my pen and fashioned a testimonial of affection in an anthology of poems that really is just a love letter to Ukraine. My greatest wish is that my friends who call Ukraine their home will be validated, comforted, and encouraged by this offering of love.

Becoming Ukraine

A little boy in a striped coat stumbles and cries

walking toward the border.

A man in a military uniform

lifts his son into his arms

to say goodbye

kissing him and hugging him

as the throng loads for Poland.

The baby shouts a feeble "no…"

and beats Daddy's helmet

in protest of their parting

as an endless stream of women

and children are separated

from the men

by the glass of the railcar windows.

It begins to rain

and mingle with tears

either side of the glass

as little hands press against the pane.

Daddy starts running

to keep their hands touching

until the speed of the train

parts father from son

for "just a while"

or maybe for an eternity.

I realize I am weeping

and flashing back

to the Sunday night

at hospice

when my father

rose up to walk

in newness of life

and my hand tried

to stop the rain

from running down the glass

as my heart whispered,

"Daddy, come back."

Suddenly,

I am every child

beating Daddy's chest

to make him get on the

train with Momma.

I am the boy walking

and wailing in grief

as blisters rub on his feet

as he heads alone

to the Polish border.

I am every mother

lifting her child's shirt

to write on precious skin

the phone numbers,

names, and addresses

of every relative

she can think of,

and then,

her own identification numbers

on the child's arms,

and in turn,

the child's info

on her own arms

in case they are separated.

I am the little boy in Bucha

who takes his lunch

and lays it

on his mother's grave

so she doesn't get hungry.

I am a young mother

in Mariupol

trapped in a basement

with no water.

I nurse my baby

though I am dehydrating.

Eventually I am lifeless

and my baby

is my love song

to Ukraine.

I watch these newsreels

coming from Europe

and I am crushed

and reconstituted.

I fall into an open grave

proud to lie with

my brave countrymen.

I watch the news

and my soul bursts

over the barriers of my eyes

running down my face

a flash flood of grief

lifting my heart

and swirling it around

in a whirlpool of despair

here on my side

of the world

on this side

of the television screen

with its half-news

and obscenity of knowing.

I have no right

to these tears

here in my safe

and unaffected life.

I do not live

these obscenities.

These war crimes

did not visit my home

and tear my flesh

and so I have no right

to be comfortable

and cry the tears

that belong to those

standing by

a fallen loved one

Or an open grave

Or to someone

sitting next to their child

wondering how they can

bury them and when

and, until then,

will sit to protect

them from the jackals.

Who am I,

to sob and cry

as if this were my soul

torn from its bed?

Who am I

to cry out

at the injustice

I have never felt?

To weep for children

to whom I never gave life?

I have hijacked their pain

and made it my own

and think I know grief.

But I do not.

And so I must pay.

And pay I shall.

In words of witness

and honor.

Words that cry out

speaking truth to power

and indifference

and dismissal.

Words that will

not be ignored.

Words that mark

the days

and the places

and the souls

evil visited

and violated

in their homes

and ate its belly full

while the rest of the world

turned its head

saying it was too much.

Too much.

TOO MUCH?

For who?

Is it too much

for you

with your remote control?

Or too much

for the men

who dug their own graves?

To the mother

who gave herself

to a group of demons

to save her children

from violation?

Hoping her husband

would be allowed to live.

It was not too much for her!

She walked into death and destruction

like an angel of God

knowing who she was

and laying down her life

because there was no greater

love than hers.

We have no right

to look the other way.

We have no right

to cover the photos

and reels and

say they violate

Facebook's community standards

and are not from reliable sources.

We have no right

to weep

as if our own souls

are tearing open

and spilling on the floor.

Not if we turn

and walk away

and go eat a hot meal

and enjoy a fresh drink of water

and sleep safely in bed.

We who do not lie awake

next to our helpless children

listening for the sound of missiles.

We have no right

Unless we stop

and open our eyes

and call to others

to witness and respond

and do something

to send light into darkness.

Heat into cold.

Medicine to sickness.

Food to hunger.

The Lord our God

to face the EVIL

that is roaming their land.

Once you have stopped

and looked

and actually done something

to honor those

who laid down their lives

in Mariupol,

Bucha,

Dnipro,

Irpin,

Donetsk,

when you do something

to help those they died to save,

then you may come

sit with me

and weep.

We will open

the reservoir of our hearts

and let them release

a million tears of despair

to wash down our faces

and through our souls

rushing to the feet of Christ

where we bow down

and beg for forgiveness

and help

and salvation.

Salvation for those rising up

to live every day in service

to their homeland

their kinsmen

their God.

When you have poured yourself out

at the throne of God

on behalf of Ukraine,

come weep with me

and then we will humbly

share pictures and videos

and say…

"Here is my brave friend..."

"Here is their beautiful homeland..."

"Look at the soul…"

"Feel the heartbeat…"

"Of our precious Ukraine."

Eternal Bloom

Toss me into an open grave

Thank God you ran out of body bags

For who would wish to rot alone in a sterile
plastic bag?

No, toss me in with my kinsmen

Put us all together

Let us mingle

And become part of one another

We've earned that right…

Running out to block the tanks

Evacuating under hails of bullets

Shielding the children as best we could

Our awkward bodies made swift and sure by love

Lay me down among my kinsmen

That we may ever share

Our love of Ukraine,

Our love for each other

When you've filled us in

Covered us over

With the blessed soil

Of our motherland

Plant sunflowers in the churchyard

And here, just over our heads,

Remember to come loyally

Planting tulip bulbs each year

That we may offer ourselves

As sweet gifts of spring

In unending renewal

Then cut a bouquet

Make me your guest

Arranging me at your kitchen table

That I may live forever

Abiding at home

Remember us

But do not leave us

Fallen and forgotten

Here in the ground

Gather us in your arms

Each new spring

Take us to church on Easter

At every celebration of life

Let me grow again and again

Beneath the sod

My heart cries out

One last sacred prayer

Let me bloom forever

Amid my kinsmen

In my beloved

Ukraine.

Mariupol Mother

Forgive me, my child

For I am waning

I have loved you more

More than life

More than myself

Remember that I loved you

With all there was of me

In this dark basement

I gave you my light

I gave myself

Here in this basement

Beyond the terror

My light and life are now yours

My beloved child

My beloved country

Go with Mother Ukraine

She will feed you

She will love you

Drink of her light

Drink of her life

My love now shines in your eyes

My heart will sing in your smile

My peace rests in your heartbeat

My beloved son

God will shine on you again

You shall see the sun and sky

Drink of fresh water

And grow strong

Strong as Ukraine

I'll be that star you see

Shining brighter than the rest

Delighting to see my son

Free of darkness and

In loving arms…

The loving arms of Ukraine.

Song of My Mother

In the blink of an eye

The drop of a bomb

You are with me

In small ways

That take me back

To when there was no war

No hate

No pain

Death did not exist

And you were never older than I am now

And strong, always strong

Lending me your hope

Giving me your faith

That the world was worth saving

Steps were worth taking

Grabbing my hand

And running to take cover

And then singing

You sang in the dark

The songs that must be sung

Soft as a bird

Or mighty as the sea

Faith must roar on and

Sing in our hearts

They lay you

In this open grave

With a thousand other countrymen

Your song rises

From the trench

Sounding revelry

Calling to my soul

"Run!

Hide!

Survive!

Live on!

Remember me

And sing my song

Soft as bird

Mighty as the sea

Sing and remember me!"

You are with me in small ways

In the song of the bird

In the roar of the sea

You sing inside of me

My mother

My Ukraine

Heroes In The Doorway

There are heroes who fall in battle, and heroes who fall in the doorway.

I get my news from Alexandr. I am not sure if I spelled that right, so let's just call him Sasha. He spends loads of time rescuing people, running missions of mercy, and saving souls in the middle of bullets and bombs and a world gone mad. And since the US has decided we don't really need to know what horrors are befalling those I love in Ukraine, I check in with Sasha on social media a lot. I always get the updates a day or two early as he posts official bomb, missile, and drone counts of the day. He always shows me videos of the unbearable sadness dished out during the night in places close to where he or his friends live. So today, when I checked in, he had posted a photo that was not gruesome to see, but gruesome to feel. Because before you even learn what souls inhabited the room, you can read between the slats of the baby crib and know someone as precious as gold is missing from the room.

The shattered room's curtains are drifting in the wind like fingers pointing to the crib. The clean crib has no signs of damage, no tell-tale blood, but all around, life is shattered.

Someone has padded it all the way around with thick cushions and pillows. Across the crib's top a jigsaw puzzle of pillows and stuffed toys cover the inhabitants leaving small cracks allowing for air. This barrier protects against flying glass, falling plaster and scattering shrapnel. These top cushions are slightly disturbed as you would imagine they would be had someone pulled the baby out. Or as in this case, two babies.

I look at this photo thinking about the love it took to engineer the little cave of safety, but before I see Sasha's caption, a sadness and dread wash over me. I realize Sasha would not be showing this photo if all was well with the souls of this home. I study the crib and see no signs of devastation in the crib, only all around it. Tears stream down my face as I realize the one who created the little cove of safety in the crib is this photo's subject. The missing parent. The fallen parent.

With my stomach in the same knot it has been in for the past two years, I scrolled up to read Sasha's details.

The mother is lying sacrificed just beyond in the doorway.

Shifting the protective wall around them and stopping in the doorway to say a prayer for her babies, she takes one last look and turns toward household chores as the explosion shatters their world. Her labors of love now ended, she lies in the doorway as rescue comes.

In an answer to all her prayers, the babies are taken to safety in loving arms not her own. A Ukrainian blessing granting the wish of every mother for the salvation of their children.

By now they have planted her in the gentle Ukrainian soil and the blood of fallen soldiers has begun to water her heart. Her children are already growing from the seed of who she was and will grow tall under a blue Ukrainian sky with their faces turned toward the sun. Her sacrifice in the nursery's doorway is rewarded in her children as they walk through fields of flowers feeling the heartbeat of the soul who loved them more than life.

There are heroes who fall in battle, and heroes who fall in the doorway.

Peace Perfect Peace

Pink curtains float in the settling debris and
wave lazy fingers toward the crib.

Sirens scream in the distance as moonlight fills
this little nursery flooding in through the missing
wall.

As a pile of cushions in a baby's crib sway ever
so slightly, a whisper

   "Peace…"

drifts over the room as a tall man emerges next
to the crib. His robes glow as he softly shifts a
teddy bear lying on top of the crib and stoops to
whisper again…

   "Peace…"

The pillows grow still and the small sweet
sounds of a baby's slumber drift around the
room. The man smiles and glows brighter as he
lays his hand across his heart and then across the
top rail of the crib.

Turning from the crib, a brighter radiance washes over him as he stops in the doorway to kneel next to a fallen woman. He tenderly wipes a splatter of blood from her cheek and picks up her hand. Her eyes flutter open as he rises and draws her up to stand with him. She looks down to the fallen mother where she lies in the doorway and back to him as he nods and softly speaks…

"Peace."

She moves as if to step into the room. He lays a hand on her shoulder as shouts erupt and running footsteps ascend the stairwell, stepping right through them, to attend to the fallen mother on their way into the shattered nursery. A baby startles beneath the pile of pillows and begins to wail.

She begins to glow and he holds her back from the room…

" Let them answer your
    prayer…"

The rescue workers reach through the pile of pillows and toys to pull out not one, but two grieving babies. Their wails are muffled as the rescue workers each cradle a baby against their chest. More men appear and pick up the fallen mother from the doorway.

As the men descend the stairs, He holds her hand keeping her with him.

> "Peace…" echoes down the stairwell and covers the rescue squad.

> "Your prayers have been answered, and it is time to go."

He leads her through the shattered nursery stopping at the crib to reach in and pull out a little teddy bear. The bear begins to glow. He hands her the bear and guides her through the rubble to the missing wall. He waits as she hugs the bear and begins to grow brighter and brighter until the room fades and only a blue Ukrainian sky waits before them.

She looks at him as a smile finds her face.

> "Peace?" she asks.

> "Perfect peace," a smile spreads across his face as he answers back.

Their voices echo across the heavens as they
step together into the blue…

" Peace!"

Her Heart, Their Home

She stops her car alongside the road near a forest somewhere in Ukraine. She gathers bags and pots and pans and slowly carries them into the woods where the peace is almost magical. Setting her wares down on a path, she softly calls into the foliage. Timid ears creep up dragging cautious sets of eyes with them as these forgotten angels look to see if it is safe to emerge. And suddenly tails wag and wiggle and break into a run to greet the angel in jeans and a puffer jacket.

Sporting the collars loving families placed around their necks before Putin forced their families to leave them behind because there were more children than they could carry or an invalid parent that had to be transported. Or, sadness of all sadness, their masters were captured or killed. They wear their collars like family crests to remember those that loved them and once called them their own. Proud to carry on for their family and praying heaven will bring them back again.

They have made a family of themselves here in their forest where they hide, careful to garner no attention, and wait for Ann to return with food, medicine, and affection.

She appears and calls with words of love to let them know the coast is clear and there is food for their bodies and souls. Amazingly, they wait their turn until she has finished dishing out the porridge and passing out the raw meat she has found in town. If they are lucky, she has seen volunteers or found some money to buy dog food and today they will have some extra nutrition to face the cold winter night.

On really good days she has veterinarian tablets to help keep them healthy as if they were her very own dogs.

As they eat, she takes a place along the forest trail and sits patiently waiting for them to fill their bellies. And when they have eaten all they can hold, they come to her to have their canine souls nourished with the affection they crave more than food.

She assures each one he is a good boy and gives them a hug and a rub behind the ears to let them know she really means it. She rubs their tummies and loves each as if they were her own.

Then she gathers her dishes and bags and carries them to her car before nightfall.

Later, her fur babies, her tails, will lie down in a bed of leaves deep in the foliage and dream of home and hugs and tummy rubs.

Ann Nazarenko works professionally with displaced mothers and their children. Her office hours are full of the important business of holding Ukraine together. The rescue teams rendering aid all around Ukraine know her by name, not so much because she is beautiful, and she is beautiful, but because she leaves no soul behind. She helps the local veterinarian and drives to abandoned and bombed-out houses taking care of helpless kittens and old dogs who hide in plain sight because they don't know where to go. Their healthy condition is testimony to her faithfulness. No ribs are showing. There are no sunken eyes or draining noses. Every lost dog and kitten looks like they have a home. And I suppose if they could talk, they would tell you,

"Yes, yes, we do have a home. Right there, inside her heart."

God and Stas

God is on night watch

Doing duty in Ukraine

With his servant Stas

Fools at War

Bombs flash in God's eyes

His heart hears babies cry

And wrath fills the skies

Cast of Clowns

There is a cast of clowns

In Moscow tonight

Making plans to bomb my friends

Launching drones and missiles

Like a carnival show

Killing people without end

But the idiot's ignorance will be his downfall

As the bombs flash in God's eyes

He notes every strike in every place

Each is printed on His heart

Every man, woman, dog, cat, and child

He will avenge every soul who

Relies on his unchanging grace

The clown has to be ignorant about God

Loving his own

He knows when each one falls

He has prepared for them His home

His wrath boils over like lava

When He decides, He will let it flow

There'll be no safe place to hide

In the streets of Moscow

Just keep clowning around

Flashing Ukrainian skies

With drones and missile strikes

Blinding God in the eyes

Send them right to his heart

Time and time again

You'll learn most horrifically

God's enemies never win

New Math

As much as I despise Putin,

Multiply that times all the words of Jesus Christ

and I come out loving Ukraine

like life itself.

You take Evil, and you blast it all over Ukraine

and the people of Ukraine take it

and twist it and use it to love each other even

more. They find a way to love

more than their hearts can hold. They find a way

to give out of nothing but the love of God.

 It's like Ukrainian Math.

One Evil Tyrant slaughters and kills everything

beautiful he finds. Homes and churches and
schools are reduced to rubble.

Multiply that by 2 years and what

do you have? Stronger Ukrainians with more

love than ever working harder than

ever giving more of themselves than ever. Acts

of love and compassion for each other more than

Mr. Putin can count or even imagine.

The blood of the soldiers water the fields of

Ukraine with their kindness in war like

when they stopped and rescued kittens and

puppies and shared with them

what little rations they had.

Every soldier's grave echos with the sound of a

violin that was once played

beside a battlefield fox hole keeping them sane

and civilized and humane as barbarians took
their aim.

Keep your data charts and study your war, but I

know God's math and the

numbers run differently with him.

PUTIN× 2 YEARS = God's Wrath boiling like a

molten lava God is waiting to pour all

over the Kremlin

UKRAINE × 2 years = God's affection growing

more and more for the people of the

land as they turn to God and learn how to bring

light out of darkness, love out of hate,

hope out of fear, peace out of chaos

Do the math.

Dreams

Take me to a basement in Mariupol so I may
hear a Mother sing a lullaby to Ukraine.

Run me through the Carpathian Mountains so
that I can look down on the rolling grandeur
across the land.

I want to see Dnipro and Irpin and the patriots
old and stooped and too broken in body to run
but refusing to leave their land for strangers to
pillage. I wish to kiss them on the cheek and
wish them God's peace and mercy.

Take me to Kiev to study the gospel and then on
to Lviv to restore my joy with the fellowship of
saints.

I want to drive down to Chernivtsi and see
where the brotherhood slept elbow to elbow
keeping warm and slipping into slumber to the
symphonic tones of competitive snoring.

Let me ride with Sasha and Bohden to the
marketplace below ground to buy boxes of
sustenance and carry them on a mission of

mercy stopping to see lonely children along the way.

Take me up into the mountains to the peace that waits there. We will walk the dog and drive back to the church at sunset.

Show me what still stands of Odessa and let me listen to the hope of the ocean.

Let me listen to the wives of brave men explain how their husbands saved all those lives and managed to keep everyone well through the hardest winter. Secrets. Tell me the secrets of how they loved the church through the long impossible winter.

For I am starved for a language I cannot understand. I am desperate to see faces I would recognize anywhere and feel them reach out and hold my face and say " Oh! There you are! At last! Our friend from Texas! So this is you? Welcome to our hearts."

I do not understand all the ways of God except that the blood of Jesus Christ is a miracle tonic that brings life, and love, and fellowship in small packages from far away and multiplies them just like the loaves and fishes so that those who have only seen each other in photos and videos cultivate an admiration in Christ that grows into a mighty affection where hearts take shelter and rest for just awhile. I suppose very much like when Jesus said those of us that have not seen but believe would be blessed.

And that's the crux of the matter. We love Jesus whom we have not seen and that makes the Jesus in me love the Jesus in you. I long for the day I see Jesus Christ face to face. Sometimes that longing hurts because it grows within me until I can no longer stand it and it drives me to search for Jesus where I can find him inside of you.

Yes, you. I see and delight in little bits and pieces of Him that have fallen through the cracks of your soul and landed in your heart to spark a light that beams so brightly out of your eyes that I don't need to speak Ukrainian to experience Jesus Christ in you.

A great despair washes over me when I realize I am not able to see Ukraine in person. Its beauty and majesty are things I'll have to view one day through heaven's windows. And to think I will never embrace the brothers and sisters of faith

who have grown to occupy so much space in my
heart makes me weepy at times.

But if I cannot go to Ukraine, then one day, and I
really mean this, one day, I am determined to
show up on the doorstep at the Tuscumbia
Church where I fully expect to be greeted by
Jeff Abrams with open arms and a generous
mind so that I may bask in the presence of so
many brave Ukrainians who have endured an
exodus and are making their way in a strange
land with some mighty strange people. They are
my heroes.

So take me to Tuscumbia where I can celebrate
the mystery of Christ with my friends Bohdan
and Viktor and their amazing wives. I'll listen to
the boys' tales of school and football and how
that marvelous Dnipro kicker, Bohden The
Younger, has already landed in big photos in the
newspapers!

I want to see how outrageously tall Damir has
grown in his big-boy pants. For I am homesick
for my brothers and sisters from a land I have
not known yet held like precious gold deep in
my heart.

I just want a little taste of Ukrainian Heaven to hold me over until I see my savior face to face.

If that is too much to ask, I will learn to grow content with my dreams. For I do dream almost every night, if just for a little while, of the beauty of Ukraine.

Precious, heavenly Ukraine.

The Lviv Diet

That McDonald's sack

Drive-thru each day for a month

Would keep my friends warm

Trust

Daddy died

My dog crossed the rainbow

Stage 4 Cancer

I learned to pray

And sleep at night by trusting Him

And face the new morning

It's time I trusted God with Ukraine

Said my prayers, loosened my grip

And went to sleep.

(Ironically, I got this idea from a

friend in Ukraine.)

Wings

Weary wings soaring

Seeking a forever space

Peace must find her home

Sweet Peace

Hush sweet bird of Peace

Take cover and rest and mend

Some day you'll be home

Peace In The Doorway

She landed in my doorway

And leaned against the frame

Feathers singed and ruffled

Ashes filling her eyes with pain

She'd traveled so many miles

Soaring sea to sea

Searching for a place to nest

She finally came to me

I saw the world in her eyes

Cities, mountains, towns

She'd searched the whole world over

But a home she had not found.

Smoke of burning buildings

Dust of fallen bombs

Clung to her pure white soul

And choked her lovely song

I washed the war off of her wings

Rinsed the death out of her eyes

She took her ease upon my pillow

And slept until the sunrise

I shared what I had with her

Offered her my home

She sang a song of gratitude

But I knew she must be gone

She made her way to my doorstep

I prayed she'd be alright

For she's much ground to travel

Before she ends her flight

Peace must find a forever home

Not just now and then

She longs for a space to call her own

Within the hearts of men

I wept to see her go

Then paused and turned around

To see the gift she had left for me

An olive branch on the ground

Fly high my sweet dove of Peace

You've very far to roam

But one day man will learn to love

And you'll finally have your home.

Peace landed in my doorway...

Finding Home

Why must the Dove of Peace live without her
mate?

Why does she roam alone?

Searching for a humble nest

To finally make her home?

Why not help her breed Peace?

By the nest full here to there?

Make a world where she can soar

And see her children everywhere

Children who study peace

And soar on wings of love

Whose songs rise to the heavens
As praise to Him above

Why can't Peace find a mate

Within the heart of men?

Find a home among the nations

And sing her song again

This world will grow sick of pain

And the practice of evil ways

I pray day and night within my life

We live to see the days

When Peace sings a joyful song

No longer forced to roam

She'll make her nest of the olive branch
And every heart her home

Putin's Folly

Putin's problem now

Martyrs' bloodstains won't wash off

Without Jesus Christ

Nightingale

A nightingale sings in the courtyard
A song of loss and pain.
I stand between your headstones
And whisper "Slava Ukraine."

"She sings me back to memories
Of a night now long passed
The longest night, the sacred night,
The night that was your last.

"Remember everything I told you…"
Papa pulled down the attic stairs sending me out
of sight.
He closed the trap door and I covered it
With a rug to block all light.

"I love you!" Mama called out
As the soldiers broke down the door.
I rolled to the corner of the outside wall
Just like we'd practiced before.

Silent as a church mouse
I covered my lips just so
Holding back my angry cries
At the unholy sounds below.

First a crash and then a scream
A shot beyond the hall
Mama cried, and then she sobbed
Then made no sound at all.

The demons crash around taking things
Defiling our little house.
The rusty spring moaned on the courtyard gate
When they cursed their way back out.

Papa had taught me not to move
Until I'd said "The Lord's My Shepherd…"
times three.
I finished my prayers and climbed back down
to search for my family.

Mama's clothes were torn away
Her hair pulled out of place.
I pulled the dress back around her
Smoothed her hair and kissed her lovely face.

Her beautiful blue eyes were frozen
In a gaze so soft and sweet
Resting where her love lay
Just beyond her reach.

Papa had a hole where his heart should have
been
And blood soaked his sweater vest.

His eyes were locked on Mama
Where they ever more shall rest.

I took his calloused hand in mine
And reached for Mama's too
Cherishing the last warmth they had
Remembering their love once new.

A sanguine river ran from Mama
And met with Papa's blood.
I sat there by the stream
An endless flowing love.

In the courtyard a nightingale sang
A song of loss and pain.
I hung my head as my tears flowed down
Like gentle summer rain.

I slipped Mama's ring from her finger
Laid her hand back on her chest
Took Papa's from his callused hands
His watch from within his vest.

I slid the rings on the watch's chain
And latched its loop shut tight
Then kissed my Papa on his cheek
And straightened up his tie.

"Dear Papa, I'll never forget

The things you've taught me
To love my country, and my home,
And always to live free."

The sun came up, as it always does.
I washed my face and hands
Put on the clean shirt Mama had pressed
And donned my trouser pants.

I slid the watch into my pants' pocket
And felt the rings once more.
I whispered," I love you," one last time
Stepped bravely out the door.

On the street, the neighbors praised
And hugged our army men.
I saw one wearing a Trident spear,
And I took him by the hand.

He looked down and kindly asked
"Good son, have you need of me?"
So I led him to Mama and Papa
Where he could plainly see.

He turned his misty eyes to mine
And I saluted through my pain,
"Tis my Mama and my Papa, sir.
All glory to Ukraine!"

The nightingale sings in the courtyard
Amid the roses sweet.
The soldiers helped me plant them there
When we laid you beneath the peat.

The Lord is my shepherd, Mama,
He gets me through the pain,
But I wear the Trident for Papa now.

"Slava Ukraine."

SLAVA PAPA

Soft rain leaves tears on the train's window.
Where do they come from, the stars or me?
Or your whispers, "My love, I have to go,"
As you dropped your arms leaving mine empty.

I begged the stars to send you back again
To sing a lullaby and dry my tears
Run off the monsters, chase away the rain
Show me how to live now that you're not here.

The sweater that you left is so chilling.
Your photo says I am now all alone.
In this noisy crowd, silence is killing.
My heart screams to me " Run all the way
home!"

But walk my dreams softly, whisper all night
Hold me, dear Papa, and I'll be alright.

Ukrainian Promise

Rain, rain, rain, thank God for sending this rain
And hiding all my tears
A tiny hand reaches mine through the pane

He believed me when I said we'd meet again
His face so sadly severe
Filled my heart with grief and pain

That I'd lied again and again in hopeful refrain
To give him some cheer
Now that lie's a promise I must attain

I run with you, son, beside the train
And promise you, my dear,
My heart will beat for you, my life will sustain

Run, now, with your mother, do not complain
Keep her ever very near
Help her play to win this little hiding game.

I vow to you now I will not be slain
Nor be swallowed up in this cold terrain
We'll live again free from fear
In our home, this home, our beloved Ukraine.

A Dumbass* in the Donbass

*Dumbass: Noun. A stupid or contemptible
person or leader. Sometimes both.

Get your dumb ass
Out of the Donbass.

The more you pillage
The more you rape
The more you kill
And kidnap

The more they cry
Out to God
The more they rush
To care for each other.

The more you disgrace
Your own people
The more honor
Ukraine shows the world.

Your drones
Your bombs
Your missiles
Have missed their mark.

Their mothers
Their fathers
Their children
Live forever in their hearts.

And nothing you do
Can stop them from
Believing in their homeland
And each other.

The waters rage
As does the wrath of God.
The fires burn
As does the vengeance of God.

As a dumbass in the Donbass
You know nothing of God.
While you destroy your own
God defends His own.

The mighty right arm of God is bare
As he rolls up his sleeves
To avenge His people
As you fan the fires of His rage.

No army
Marching against God
Has ever seen victory.
He will make the crooked

Straight.

Ukraine has loved its neighbors
While you have loved yourself.
Wake up and smell the coffee.
Read the writing on the wall.

"God opposes the proud
But gives grace to the humble."

Your time runs short
To get your dumb ass
Out of the Donbass.

Ukrainian Sky

The sky holds my daddy
In its arms
Keeping him safe for me.

The sun keeps Daddy's smile
In its vault
Keeping him warm for me.

The moon and Daddy laugh
Through the night
Keeping him happy for me.

Stars shine like Daddy's eyes
Blinking and winking
Keeping him near to me.

The sky holds my daddy
In its arms
Keeping him safe for me.

Loving Ukraine

When I was 12, I fell in love

With a town called Anatevka

Now I have friends there

I get up in the dead of the night

To worship with them

And break bread with them

Lviv stole my heart

And hung it on their Christmas tree

Just in time to make my holidays

Merry and bright

Chernivtsi taught me joy

When I thought myself

Poor in spirit

And believed

I'd never dance again

The preacher, Dmytro,

Forgives me

For calling him "Frank"

And always lends me his smile

Even though I never

Spell his name right

Victor inspires me with how he loves

His dog and cat

So much, in fact,

He gave up his freedom

To keep them safe and

Found a place where

They all serve God

Ann saves every lost pet she finds

And has salvaged my heart

Along the way

The Volunteer Brothers

Are my superheroes

Here in America

My friends and I refer to them as

"The Bad Donkey Christians"

Only we don't say "donkey"

We use the Biblical word

That starts with an "a"

But my grandmother

Won't give me gum

And a new box purse

If I type that word right now

How about Adi Voicu

From Romania

Turning all things to joy

With all that smiling

By the skin of his teeth

Running through the Carpathians

Like he's joyriding with a

Thousand gallons of gasoline

Bouncing around the trailer

Alexandr? Fearless.

Absolutely fearless.

Children without parents

People without homes

Souls needing to find their God

He goes to them all

With bombs falling everywhere

He follows the footsteps of Jesus

And manages to dodge

All the bullets and bombs

He also navigates sadness

He and Stas

Have a gift for navigating

Sadness and fear

At every bend in the road

They flip it upside down

And turn it into joy

Everywhere they go

I am suspicious

There's a sort of magic

In their smiles

That they borrowed

From The Savior

That would explain it

What's really great

Is Jeff Abrams

Has brought enough

Ukrainians to Tuscumbia

That, if we are lucky,

Enough of their tenacity

Of hope and love

Just might rub off of them

And float around in the air

Here in America

That eventually

We will lighten up

And stop taking ourselves so seriously

That maybe, just maybe,

It'll get easier to breathe

Around this joint

Bohdan Y and Viktor

And their families

And church mates

Always leave

Joy in my heart

I have never seen people

Follow so bravely

Where the footsteps of Jesus

Have led them

Never

A good dose of Ukraine

Always makes me stronger

And leaves me with a smile

I have no idea

What the idiot

Was thinking

When he started

This war

I'm heartbroken

At all the loss

Of these past two years

But in the middle of the loss

Ukraine has a way of turning

Pain into gain

Hate into love

Chaos into order

Ashes to beauty

How can I help but to love Ukraine?

The Lighthouse

Thank you for letting me love you.

In the middle of your own crisis

you opened your hearts to me.

Across the sea, thousands of miles away,

I watched you face each challenge,

each heartbreak,

each setback

with a thoughtfully poised and tender demeanor

that advertised the love of God

and shined His light

into darkness.

You have met every crisis

with hope and love.

You have shown the world

there is a God.

You have led your countrymen

to safety.

You held up spiritual light

and showed others the way

 to navigate the madness.

The unending capacity of hope

welling up among the brethren

has been Ukraine's saving grace.

My prayer is that you always

keep that spirit among you

so that when Peace makes

its home in Ukraine once again,

the world will see

the spirit of Christ shine

brighter than ever.

Ukraine- a beacon of hope for the world.

God's Lighthouse.

www.ingramcontent.com/pod-product-compliance
Lightning Source LLC
La Vergne TN
LVHW050918200726
843508LV00011B/2222